SUPERVISING FOR SUCCESS

A Guide for Supervisors

Tony Moglia

A Crisp Fifty-Minute™ Series Book

This Fifty-Minute™ book is designed to be "read with a pencil." It is an excellent workbook for self-study as well as classroom learning. All material is copyright-protected and cannot be duplicated without permission from the publisher. *Therefore, be sure to order a copy for every training participant by contacting:*

THOMSON

COURSE TECHNOLOGY

1-800-442-7477 • 25 Thomson Place, Boston MA • www.courseilt.com

SUPERVISING FOR SUCCESS

Tony Moglia

CREDITS
Managing Editor: **Kathleen Barcos**
Editor: **Kay Keppler**
Production: **Leslie Power**
Typesetting: **ExecuStaff**
Cover Design: **Nicole Phillips**

ISBN 1-56052-460-X
Library of Congress Catalog Card Number 97-67631
Printed in Canada by Webcom Limited
4 5 6 7 PM 06 05

LEARNING OBJECTIVES FOR:

SUPERVISING FOR SUCCESS

The objectives for *Supervising for Success* are listed below. They have been developed to guide you, the reader, to the core issues covered in this book.

Objectives

☐ 1) **To discuss the attitude and image of the supervisor**

☐ 2) **To explain human skills and team building**

☐ 3) **To suggest ways to best get the work done**

Assessing Your Progress

In addition to the learning objectives above, Course Technology has developed a Crisp Series **assessment** that covers the fundamental information presented in this book. A 25-item, multiple-choice and true/false questionnaire allows the reader to evaluate his or her comprehension of the subject matter. To buy the assessment and answer key, go to www.courseilt.com and search on the book title or via the assessment format, or call 1-800-442-7477.

Assessments should not be used in any employee selection process.

About the Author:

Tony Moglia is president of Competitive Solutions, a California-based training and consulting firm specializing in communications, management, team building, customer service, and human resources training. Competitive Solutions also facilitates meetings for boards of directors, senior management, project teams, work groups, and company retreats. Tony has worked with a wide range of organizations, including Commerce Clearing House Inc., Dipaco Inc., National Semiconductor, Pete's Brewing Co., Pinkerton Security Services, Zacson Corp., and Pacific Gas & Electric, where for 15 years he served as Senior Consultant from the boardroom to the plant floor.
Competitive Solutions can be contacted at:
Phone: (510) 339-2270
Fax: (510) 339-9166

CONTENTS

v

CONTENTS (continued)

SECTION

I

A Role Defined

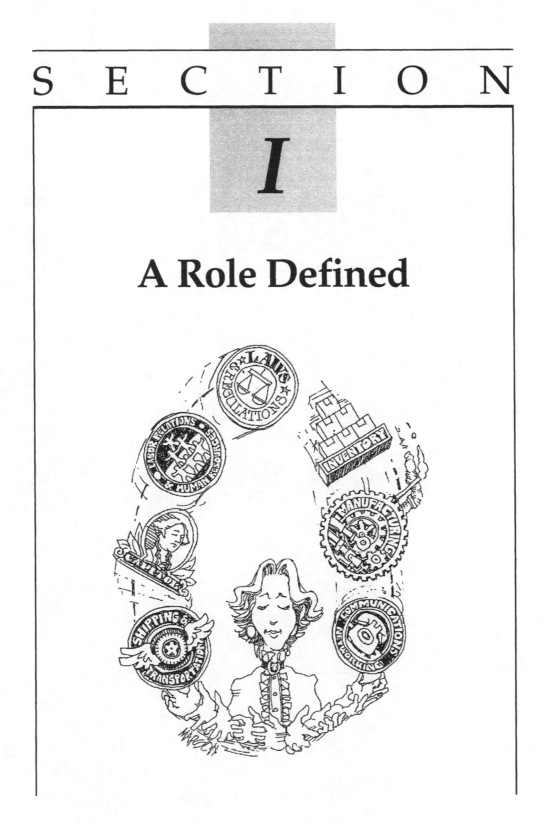

THE SUPERVISORY CHALLENGE

Supervising others is a special challenge that can help you reach new career and lifestyle goals, but becoming a successful supervisor is not as easy as some people imagine. Three factors will require that you be a different kind of person on the job.

► You will be *expected to lead* where in the past you may have been a peer member of the team. This means your employees will be watching your actions in the hope that you will make good, quick decisions that will lead your team in the best direction.

► Your role will put you in the position of *buffer between your supervisor and those you supervise.* This means you must satisfy management and, at the same time, keep your employees happy so they will maintain high productivity. At times you may have to absorb pressure from above rather than pass it on to your employees.

► You will need to *communicate your company's mission.* You will be setting standards rather than living up to those set by others. This means you will be responsible for creating a disciplined environment where employees do not violate company standards or those set by you. When violations occur, you may have to sensitively coach and counsel the rulebreakers.

All of this should be accepted as a challenge that will help you grow into a stronger person. And, of course, these challenges bring special rewards.

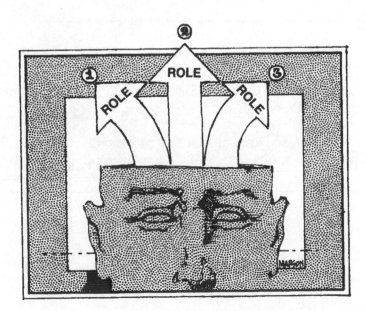

THE RESPONSIBILITIES OF SUPERVISORS

Employees have responsibilities to the company and to you, their boss. You, as a supervisor, have responsibilities as well. What are they?

► **RESPONSIBILITY TO MANAGEMENT.** You are now a member of the management team; therefore, you are expected to support management and do all you can to see that the goals of management are realized.

► **RESPONSIBILITY TO YOUR UNIT.** You represent management to your team and are therefore expected to treat each individual fairly.

► **RESPONSIBILITY TO YOURSELF.** Recognize your own limitations. In accepting the position of supervisor, you accept the responsibilities that go with the position. These will be challenging at first. If they continue to be overwhelming, consider that supervision is not for everyone. Your satisfaction and talent may lie in the front-line work, not in the managing of others.

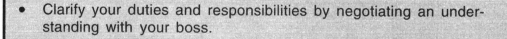

TIPS

• Clarify your duties and responsibilities by negotiating an understanding with your boss.

• Clarify the duties and responsibilities of members of your team by negotiating an understanding with each of them.

Supervisors and employees have many roles and responsibilities, which vary. Here are some of the responsibilities you may be asked to accept. Check those that apply to you.

- ❑ Scheduling
- ❑ Regulating work hours
- ❑ Observing rules compliance
- ❑ Executing disaster control plan
- ❑ Interviewing and processing new employees
- ❑ Overseeing payroll
- ❑ Monitoring vehicle and equipment inspections
- ❑ Analyzing risk management
- ❑ Writing reports
- ☑ Enforcing procedures
- ❑ Training
- ❑ Coaching and counseling
- ❑ Meeting clients
- ❑ Staffing
- ❑ Client relations
- ❑ Evaluating employees

Please add any other responsibilities you are asked to accept:

_____

_____

_____

YOUR ROLE AS SUPERVISOR

The following list summarizes the general duties of a first-line supervisor. Compare your responsibilities with this list. Are you overlooking something?

✔ **Assign and distribute work.** You set priorities on what will get done, organize the work into reasonable assignments, and then match those assignments to employees on your team.

✔ **Monitor and control performance**. To ensure that quality work is done safely and legally, you get out and see how it is done.

✔ **Review and evaluate performance.** You decide who will be recommended for promotion or pay increase, who needs coaching and counseling, and who may have to be laid off or let go.

✔ **Train and develop employees.** Your experience is a valuable resource to your team. Use problems and unusual situations as training and development opportunities. You must also see that all employees in your team are properly trained.

✔ **Lead your unit.** Leadership is demonstrated in the decisions you make, the people you hire and train, the discipline you maintain, and the example you present to your team.

✔ **Communicate.** Let your employees know what is expected, as well as policies and decisions that affect them. Notify your manager of any problems you anticipate. Advise other groups of your unit's needs and let other groups know about things your team is working on that may affect them.

✔ **Handle administrative duties.** Keep paperwork and records up-to-date. Your job will be much easier if the information you want is current and readily available.

> • *The work itself is different.*
> • *The responsibilities are greater.*

CASE STUDY #1: Who Will Survive?

Tom and Chris have both been promoted to supervisory positions, which will begin in two weeks. They are equally qualified, but they have different attitudes toward their new challenge. Which candidate stands the best chance of surviving after six months?

> The day after Tom received news of his promotion, he made a list of do's and don'ts he would follow. Tom figured he had worked under enough supervisors to know what to do. He would model his behavior on what he had learned from observation. Why bother to study techniques and principles in advance? Why get needlessly uptight by too much preparation? Tom believes personality and good common sense are all that is needed. He plans to set a good example by working hard, listening well, and staying close to the group. He will concentrate on building good relationships in all directions. Tom has complete confidence in his ability to succeed.
>
> Chris was delighted with the announcement of her promotion. She decided to use the two-week period to prepare for her new responsibilities. She found some good books on supervision and made a list of recommended techniques to follow: how to demonstrate authority, when to delegate, what changes in behavior would be required, and so on. Chris accepted the premise that she had much to learn about becoming a successful supervisor. Although she believes in herself, she does not have Tom's level of confidence. Chris has decided on the following strategy: although she intends to remain friendly and upbeat, she will slowly pull back from too much personal contact with former peers. She feels this will be necessary to demonstrate her authority. Next she will concentrate on creating a good working environment so that employees are more relaxed. Everything will be planned and orderly. Everyone will know where she or he stands and what is expected of them.

Which individual has the better chance of survival? Will Tom—with his upbeat, confident approach—do a better job than Chris with her more scientific attitude? Or will Chris—with her less confident but more deliberate strategy—survive over Tom? Check the appropriate box below.

 ❏ Tom will survive.

❏ Chris will survive.

❏ Both Tom and Chris will survive.

WHAT SUCCESS AS A SUPERVISOR CAN DO FOR YOU

Many good things can happen to you once you become a successful supervisor. Ten statements are listed below. Three are false. Place a check in the square opposite these false statements and match your answers with those at the bottom of the page. As a supervisor you may:

TRUE   FALSE

☑	☐	1. Increase your earnings potential
☑	☐	2. Have opportunities to learn more
☐	☑	3. Develop an ulcer
☐	☐	4. Position yourself for additional opportunities within your company
☐	☑	5. Have less freedom
☐	☐	6. Increase your self-confidence
☐	☐	7. Try out your leadership wings
☐	☑	8. Have fewer friends
☐	☐	9. Learn and develop human relations skills
☐	☐	10. Have greater feelings of self-worth

As you rise to the challenges of being a supervisor, it is often a good idea to model your behavior after a successful supervisor you respect. You will discover that highly successful supervisors have much in common. If the opportunity presents iteself, discuss some of the characteristics and principles of good supervision with your manager.

FALSE STATEMENTS:

3. There is no evidence that supervisors have more ulcers than non-supervisors. **5.** Supervisors normally have more freedom because they control their actions more than employees. **8.** Good supervisors develop new friends (fellow supervisors) and keep many old ones.

It is up to you to make the other statements true!

MAKE YOUR CHOICE NOW

Good supervisors come in all shapes and sizes, but they all have some characteristics in common. Compare these behaviors of successful and unsuccessful supervisors and see if you spot yourself.

SUCCESSFUL SUPERVISORS	UNSUCCESSFUL SUPERVISORS
• Remain positive under stress	• Permit problems to get them down
• Know their subject and teach employees what they know	• Offer poor instruction and follow up
• Build and maintain relationships with their employees	• Ignore employees' needs
• Delegate	• Resist learning basic supervisory skills
• Set high standards and good examples	• Fail to motivate others
• Communicate	• Let their status go to their heads
• Build team effort	• Exercise too much or too little authority

Add your own:

_____

_____

_____

_____

Add your own:

_____

_____

_____

_____

You undoubtedly have had the opportunity to study mistakes other supervisors have made. List three that you intend to avoid.

1. _____

2. _____

3. _____

SEVEN TIPS FOR GREAT SUPERVISORS

1. Be warm and friendly but establish your authority.

2. Do not play favorites. Treat each person with respect.

3. Do what you can to make everyone's job better.

4. Teach your employees new skills that will make their jobs easier.

5. Seek assistance from your manager if you hit troubled waters. Ask for suggestions. Be a good listener.

6. Give your employees credit when credit is due.

7. Do not permit former peers and co-workers to intimidate you into a wishy-washy management style.

TIPS

Employees like to know how they are doing. Take a few minutes every now and then to let your people know you appreciate their dependability and the contribution they are making. Many capable employees resign because superiors take them for granted.

You are only as good as the people who work for you. Make sure your employees regularly receive the reinforcement they need.

SECTION

II

The Attitude and Image

TAKING A POSITIVE APPROACH

Attitude is the way you approach things *mentally*. If you look at your situation positively and enthusiastically, you will communicate to those around you that you welcome the challenges and responsibilities of leadership, and everyone will enjoy working with you. If you are tentative or insecure, employees and bosses may interpret your attitude as negative, and you may receive less cooperation. You have the power to change your attitude if you don't like what it says about you. Remember, as a supervisor, everyone will be watching you. No matter what you do to hide it, your attitude will be showing.

TIPS

As you rise to the challenges of being a supervisor, it is often a good idea to model your behavior after a successful supervisor you respect.

You will discover that highly successful supervisors have much in common. If the opportunity presents itself, discuss some of the characteristics and principles of good supervision with your manager.

MEASURING YOUR MORALE

To measure your attitude, please complete this exercise. Read each statement and circle the number where you feel you belong. If you circle a 5, you are saying your attitude is the best possible in this area; if you circle a 1, you are saying supervision may not be for you.

	AGREE				DISAGREE
I seek responsibility.	5	(4)	3	2	1
Becoming a respected supervisor is important to me.	(5)	4	3	2	1
I enjoy helping others do a good job.	(5)	4	3	2	1
I want to know more about human behavior.	5	4	(3)	2	1
I want to climb the management ladder.	5	4	(3)	2	1
I am anxious to learn and master supervisory skills.	5	(4)	3	2	1
I like leadership situations.	5	(4)	3	2	1
Working with a problem employee would be an interesting challenge.	5	4	(3)	2	1
I intend to devote time to learn motivational skills.	5	4	(3)	2	1
I'm excited about the opportunity to become a supervisor.	(5)	4	3	2	1

TOTAL [   ]

If you scored higher than 40, you have an excellent attitude about being or becoming a supervisor. If you rated yourself between 25 and 40, it would appear you have a few reservations. A rating under 25 indicates you may need to pursue additional educational opportunities regarding supervision.

A POSITIVE ATTITUDE BOOSTS PRODUCTIVITY

Nothing improves relationships with those you supervise more than a consistently positive attitude on your part. Your attitude sets the pace and the tone in your team. Your tardiness will be reflected in the attitudes of your employees. Your complaints about work conditions will lower morale. Everything you do and every position you take will be reflected in the attitudes of your employees. Two expressions are appropriate. They are:

Attitudes are caught, not taught.

Your attitude speaks so loudly,
employees can't hear what you say.

Your attitude directly affects the productivity of your employees. When you are upbeat, they respond positively, and productivity increases. When you are negative, productivity drops.

WATCH YOUR CAREER SOAR

Building and maintaining healthy relationships among supervisors and co-workers is the key to success in any organization. Nothing contributes more to this process than a positive attitude.

You express your attitude before you say a word by how you look, stand, walk, and talk. If you look groomed, stand tall, walk confidently, and are cheerful and upbeat, your attitude acts like a magnet. You not only attract others, but they are more friendly toward you because they sense in advance that you already like them. When Will Rogers said, "A stranger is a friend I have yet to meet," he was expressing an attitude. Try to keep that positive attitude in the workplace.

Your co-workers appreciate a positive attitude because:

1. For many people, working is not what they would most prefer to be doing in life. Working near a positive person makes the work week more enjoyable.

2. Some people have extremely difficult private lives. Work can be a place where they can find positive people and forget about some of their problems.

3. Supervisors depend on the positive attitudes of their employees to establish a "team spirit." Positive attitudes make everyone's job a little easier.

4. Approximately half of a person's waking hours are spent in the workplace. Without some positive attitudes, this amount of time could seem endless.

Both positive and negative attitudes travel quickly. Working near a person with a positive attitude is a delightful experience. He or she can make you feel more upbeat yourself. Working near a negative person, however, can ruin anyone's day and may cause you to turn negative, which can have a disastrous effect on performance—for you and your team.

The more harmonious the environment is, the higher productivity will be. Employees will achieve more output, better quality, and fewer mistakes. When people are relaxed and happy they concentrate better and come closer to reaching their potential. A happy, productive atmosphere is traceable to the attitudes of those who create it.

Even an observant outsider can tell when a work environment is comfortable, efficient, and productive by noticing the attitudes of employees. There is more energy. Employees are more tolerant of each other. Work is viewed more as a challenge than a series of boring tasks. But beware: A single negative attitude can sour a harmonious atmosphere.

- A supervisor with a negative attitude dampens the entire operation. Nobody escapes.

- A small group of negative workers can split a team into camps. Everyone loses.

- A team can overcome the negative attitude of one employee—but it takes work!

Classifying those with positive and negative attitudes is easy when vacations roll around. The positive workers are missed and welcomed back. Negative employees give everyone else a much-needed vacation.

The point, of course, is that your positive attitude is not only priceless to you—it is also greatly valued by others!

STAYING POSITIVE TAKES EFFORT

Staying positive is not always easy. Supervisorial responsibilities are often heavy, and they can, without your realizing it, turn you negative. Make an effort to stay positive. The truth is, when you are positive, productivity is up; if you become negative, productivity drops. Your challenge is to remain positive even if those around you are not.

The exercise below assumes three things: that you are generally a positive, upbeat person; that you can take steps to remain positive; and that knowing what these steps are will help you eliminate down periods.

After reading the list, select three attitude adjusters that will do the most for you.

❑ Engage in physical exercise.

❑ Set more attainable goals.

❑ Take life less seriously.

❑ Share your positive attitude with others.

❑ Take more mini-vacations.

❑ Maintain a better balance between work and leisure.

❑ Do more to help others.

❑ Talk with a more experienced supervisor to learn how to eliminate down periods.

Others:

_____

_____

_____

_____

_____

TENDING YOUR PERSONAL GROWTH

Some supervisors get so wrapped up in their daily work that they don't attend to their personal leadership growth. Don't let yourself and your employees down. What you know and do today won't be sufficient tomorrow. You can't let personal growth slide until you "have the time." That time will never come. You must have a development plan for yourself. If you don't write it down, another crisis will take priority. Take a moment to assess your development needs and then take appropriate action.

What I Need to Know:	How I Will Learn It:	By When:
The latest trends in the landscaping industry	Attend an AIA seminar at which a landscaping industry forecaster is speaking.	mid-December

GROWING YOUR DREAM TEAM

People usually fall into one of two groups: Those who create their future, or those who let others create it. Leaders are solidly in the former group.

Leaders are never satisfied with the status quo. They always look for ways to "do things better than we do them today." True leaders seem to brim with new ideas. These ideas spring from constant scanning of the environment for trends and direction, but the focus on improvement isn't just on products or services—it's also on the people.

As a leader, an important message you should send to your employees is that everyone, regardless of experience or job title, should improve constantly. Daily work should become a constant classroom. Here are some ways to foster personal improvement.

- Attend formal off-site workshops and seminars.

- Work with employees to share insights.

- Devise group projects for cross-training.

- Visit customer locations.

- Develop or attend in-house training courses.

- Encourage special projects that enhance skills and abilities.

- Read career-related books, journals, and articles.

Whatever avenue you use, the message you send when you encourage growth is that acquiring skills and knowledge is important.

ESTABLISHING AUTHORITY

The authority to supervise your team effectively does not come automatically when you become the supervisor; you must earn it from your team. These three things will help you earn respect and authority from your team.

#1 Knowing your job

#2 Taking necessary action

#3 Dealing fairly with team members

With these qualities as a foundation, you can establish your position as supervisor.

► **GET ACQUAINTED.**

Everyone wants to know who you are and what changes to expect, and you need to know your people in order to work effectively with them.

► **MEET EVERYONE ON THE TEAM.**

Make a point during the first two or three days to meet everyone. Learn each person's background, interests, and views of the operation of the team. Share your background, philosophy on supervision, and your expectations for the team.

► **IDENTIFY INFORMAL LEADERS.**

Teaming up with the informal team leaders will help you learn the rules of the game, expectations of the team, and an understanding of its traditions. You can check out ideas you are considering to see how they might be best presented to the team. Your endorsement by informal leaders wins work-group support for you.

► **CIRCULATE AMONG TEAM MEMBERS.**

Get out of your work area and circulate among your team. This lets you see what is going on and helps you learn about the operation and any problems that exist. Members of your team will receive a sense of personal satisfaction just from the opportunity to talk to you and be acknowledged by you.

ESTABLISHING AUTHORITY (continued)

► **MINIMIZE STATUS DIFFERENCES.**

You can gain respect when you do not insist on being different from the team. Have team members call you by your first name, be accessible, and help when a crisis arises. Use your authority with discretion.

► **SET A POSITIVE TONE.**

Express your willingness and intent to get involved in whatever is necessary for the team to succeed. Establish that you and the team succeed together.

► **START SMALL.**

Establish your authority first in the most easily accepted areas around work quality and quantity and move gradually to the potentially more controversial areas such as working hours or work-group size. This approach minimizes the chances that someone will refuse your directions or challenge your authority before it is firmly established.

TIPS

- Gradually build your authority.

- Become acquainted with both the people and operations of your unit.

- Communicate clearly, directly, and confidently.

- Be persistent with your directives and requests.

There are three sources of power you can demonstrate as a supervisor:

1. Personality-Power

To understand the potential of your personality-power, you must appreciate two other primary power sources: role-power and knowledge-power. The illustration below gives personality-power the biggest segment, but don't underestimate the possible power of the other two.

2. Role-Power

Role-power comes from the position you hold. It is part of the position regardless of who occupies it. The moment someone becomes a supervisor, he or she gains power. We have all witnessed the abuse of role-power, even at the lowest level.

3. Knowledge-Power

Knowledge-power comes from understanding the skills and techniques required for good performance. As our society becomes increasingly technical and roles become more specialized, knowledge-power becomes more important.

When someone decides to build his or her skills, power sources come into play and the following considerations surface:

- How can one make sensitive use of all power sources?

- When is it best to draw power from one source rather than another?

- How does one achieve the best balance in the daily use of all three sources?

CASE STUDY #2: *Which Strategy Should Henry Use?*

> Although sensitive to the needs of fellow employees, Henry has always set higher standards for himself. He is never late, seldom absent, and, once on the job, all business. Henry attributes his work style to his upbringing and training. Henry is respected more by management than by fellow employees.
>
> Yesterday, Henry was promoted to supervisor. When informed of the promotion, Henry's manager told him: "You were selected to inspire the team to higher standards. It won't be easy, but we have faith in you, Henry."

Last night Henry sat down and developed three strategies to consider. Which one would you recommend that Henry employ?

► *Strategy 1:* Set a good example and give employees time to adjust to it.

► *Strategy 2:* Call a team meeting and explain the reason for the new expectations. Explain that the higher standards will protect jobs in the future and give employees more pride in what they are doing now. Tell them you will be consistent in holding team members accountable.

► *Strategy 3:* Do the same as Strategy 2 but on an individual coaching basis. Call in each person and explain the changes that will be made and why.

Write out your answer below.

I would recommend that Henry employ strategy #_____ for the following reasons:

_____

_____

_____

_____

See page 77 for the author's recommendation.

PRESENT A STRONG IMAGE

Supervisors should communicate a "take charge" image. They must let everyone know that things are under control—that decisions are being made and projects are moving forward. Supervisors must look comfortable in their role without giving an impression that the power has gone to their head.

Why is a stronger image necessary? First, your employees *want* you to be a leader. They will produce more if they know they are part of a cohesive group with established standards. In contrast, a weak supervisor will cause employees to be confused and unproductive.

How do you communicate a stronger image? Here are some suggestions. Place a check in the square if you agree.

❏ *Improve your appearance.* Don't overdo it, but look the part. Dress for success (shoes polished, clothes pressed, and so on).

❏ *Decide.* Make decisions with confidence. Demonstrate that you can solve problems.

❏ *Set a faster tempo.* Move about with more energy. Move with a sense of urgency. Become a model of productivity.

❏ *Handle challenges calmly.* When things go wrong, collect the facts and develop a solution. Show your inner strength. Do not display negative emotions, discouragement, or frustration in front of employees.

❏ *Share humorous incidents.* Balance your authority with a sense of humor. Help everyone have a little fun.

❏ *Demonstrate your ability to communicate with management.* Employees will feel more secure and produce more when they know you can represent them to management.

❏ *Be positive.* Communicate positively. Remember that your team's positive attitudes often depend on yours.

DOWNPLAY YOUR ROLE-POWER

As a supervisor, you have been given some authority over other employees. As a leader you may improve your value to your company by assuming that you have slightly more role-power. As a supervisor, however, you must still downplay your role-power compared to your other two power sources.

You are the designated boss, so you lead the team. Remember, however, that your personality- and knowledge-power may not yet be established. You will want to use your role power, but the power resides in the role, not the individual. Role-power is a temporary franchise. With this in mind, please check whether you agree or disagree with the following statements:

AGREE   **DISAGREE**

❏   ❏   A true leader does not need to remind team members that he or she is in charge.

❏   ❏   The more effectively you use knowledge- and personality-power, the less you will need to use role-power.

❏   ❏   The best use of role-power is to maintain discipline. Sometimes it must be used to restore structure so that everyone can reach their productivity potential.

❏   ❏   You can communicate your role-power through actions and activities.

❏   ❏   When employees respect you, they are more likely to respect the role you occupy.

❏   ❏   When someone says, "the supervisor's job has gone to his or her head," the individual means that role-power is being abused.

❏   ❏   Living with acquired role-power is difficult, especially at the beginning.

❏   ❏   Leaders who seek more role-power must learn how to use it sensitively at the beginning.

PLAY YOUR KNOWLEDGE-POWER

Many supervisors foolishly downplay knowledge as a power source. Knowledge power may be the safest and best way to demonstrate leadership. Reflect for a moment on why most people respect mentors. Isn't it because the mentor provides knowledge and guidance? If you agree, then you should strive to be both a mentor and a leader to your team. In other words, be an outstanding *teacher*. Share your knowledge.

With the above in mind, please check whether you agree or disagree with the following statements:

AGREE   DISAGREE

❏   ❏   Leaders need to be more sensitive to and generous in sharing their knowledge.

❏   ❏   Of the three sources, knowledge-power is the best way to earn respect from a team member.

❏   ❏   The more you know about your job or business, the more knowledge-power you have. Translated, this means the best use of knowledge power is to continue to learn.

❏   ❏   It is possible to overuse knowledge-power and wind up being viewed as a "know-it-all."

❏   ❏   Your personality power is the best way to communicate your knowledge-power.

❏   ❏   One need not be as sensitive in the use of knowledge-power as is true of role-power.

❏   ❏   Most supervisors and leaders have more knowledge-power than they realize, thus they tend to underuse it.

❏   ❏   Practical experience is an excellent way to gain more knowledge-power.

WHAT YOU DON'T SAY SPEAKS LOUDLY, TOO

Think about the following elements of nonverbal communication and observe the people in your team. Pledge that you will make *your* nonverbal communication say "professional."

- ► **HANDSHAKE.** Both men and women should develop a firm, steady handshake. This gesture shows self-confidence and a willingness to communicate.

- ► **APPROPRIATE LAUGHTER.** Laughter is a very individual trait, but in general, curtail loud laughter and giggling in a business setting.

- ► **FACIAL EXPRESSIONS.** Rolling your eyes and mimicking others can be interpreted as insulting.

- ► **POSTURE.** The professional person looks calm and relaxed, yet ready for work and challenge. Stand, sit, and move with positive energy.

- ► **GESTURES.** Emphasize your point when appropriate, but too many gestures can make other people uncomfortable.

- ► **EYE CONTACT.** Maintain eye contact with the person to whom you are speaking. If you are sitting, turn around and face the person fully.

ABOVE ALL—BE ORGANIZED

Presenting a strong, professional image and paying attention to your verbal and nonverbal communication are important to your success as a supervisor. Being organized is another skill that will affect your success. Some individuals fail in the role of supervisor because they are poor organizers. They are unable to organize themselves or their teams, and move from one activity to another without a plan. They assign work randomly without giving employees a chance to finish one assignment before a second is due.

Result?

Employees become frustrated, insecure, and unproductive.

The Answer?

Set daily goals as outlined in Section IV.

SECTION

III

Human Skills and
Team Building

THE BEST AND WORST SUPERVISORS

Someone once said that when you become a supervisor, you stop doing real work. In a way that's true, because now you rely on others to do the front-line work. Management is the process of getting people to do things. It's an influencing and thinking function.

Almost everybody has a story of the worst supervisor they ever knew. People can also give you an example of the best supervisor they ever knew. Not surprisingly, there are distinct differences. Usually it's easy to spot a poor supervisor or an excellent one.

In the exercise on the next page, identify the best supervisor you ever knew. What did he or she do that made him or her the best? What behaviors or characteristics describe that supervisor? List the traits on the next page.

Think of the worst supervisor you ever knew. What did he or she do that made him or her the worst? What behaviors or characteristics describe that supervisor? List the traits on the next page.

EXERCISE

Best Supervisor Behaviors or Characteristics

1. _____

2. _____

3. _____

4. _____

5. _____

Worst Supervisor Behaviors or Characteristics

1. _____

2. _____

3. _____

4. _____

5. _____

Key Assumptions

► We know a poor or excellent supervisor when we see one.

► We know a poor or excellent supervisor by our experiences with one.

► We know poor or excellent supervisors by what they do or don't do.

► Excellent supervisors are made, not born.

► We can learn to do what the best supervisors do.

SKILLS FOR SUCCESS: TECHNICAL, INTERPERSONAL, AND CONCEPTUAL

Many supervisors and managers do not see the differences between technical, interpersonal, and conceptual skills and how these skills apply to their position. Think of these skills.

► **TECHNICAL SKILLS**—Ability to use knowledge, methods, and equipment to perform tasks.

► **INTERPERSONAL SKILLS**—Ability and judgment in working with people, including an understanding of motivation and leadership.

► **CONCEPTUAL SKILLS**—Ability to understand the complexities of the entire organization and where one's team fits into the total picture.

Frontline supervisors need considerable technical skill because they are often required to train and develop new employees. Senior managers do not need to know how to perform all the tasks at the operational level, but they should understand how all the functions are interrelated. The common denominator—crucial at all levels—is interpersonal relations skill.

As supervisors move up in management, they must learn to delegate jobs requiring technical skill to their subordinates, to give themselves time to learn the interpersonal and conceptual skills now required of them.

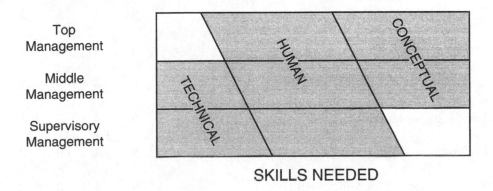

SKILLS NEEDED

SUPERVISORY SKILLS INVENTORY

What do the best supervisors do?

What do the worst supervisors do?

Participants at supervisory leadership seminars were asked these questions. The participants were mostly supervisors or people who wanted to be supervisors. They consistently expressed similar views. The Supervisory Skills Inventory came from their most-often listed behaviors of the best and worst supervisors.

Rate yourself in these areas on a scale of 1 to 5 (1 = the worst; 5 = the best). Step outside yourself and rate yourself as you think others within your company would rate you. You have nothing to lose and much to gain by being honest.

The Supervisory Skills Inventory

		BEST				WORST
1.	Gives constructive feedback	5	4	3	2	1
2.	Gives positive strokes	5	4	3	2	1
3.	Is trustworthy and ethical	5	4	3	2	1
4.	Is diplomatic	5	4	3	2	1
5.	Offers support	5	4	3	2	1
6.	Listens well	5	4	3	2	1
7.	Shows sensitivity	5	4	3	2	1
8.	Sets clear expectations and goals	5	4	3	2	1
9.	Leads by example	5	4	3	2	1
10.	Follows through	5	4	3	2	1
11.	Displays good technical ability	5	4	3	2	1
12.	Is strong but approachable	5	4	3	2	1

		BEST			**WORST**	
13.	Exhibits flexibility	5	(4)	3	2	1
14.	Makes decisions and acts	5	(4)	3	2	1
15.	Learns constantly	(5)	4	3	2	1
16.	Teaches effectively	5	(4)	3	2	1
17.	Appreciates others	(5)	4	3	2	1
18.	Is sincere and genuine	(5)	4	3	2	1
19.	Is well-organized and purposeful	(5)	4	3	2	1
20.	Delegates	5	(4)	3	2	1
21.	Achieves consistent results	5	(4)	3	2	1
22.	Is confident	5	(4)	3	2	1
23.	Demonstrates fairness	5	(4)	3	2	1
24.	Stays positive about company	5	(4)	3	2	1
25.	Expects excellence	5	(4)	3	2	1
26.	Takes reasonable risks	5	(4)	3	2	1

TOTAL [   ]

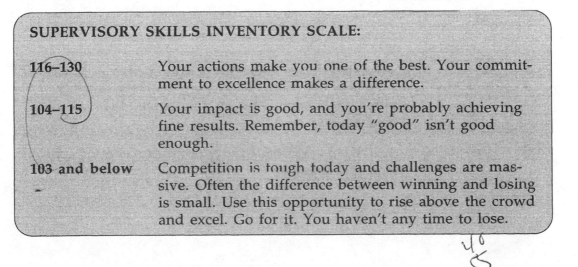

SUPERVISORY SKILLS INVENTORY SCALE:

116–130	Your actions make you one of the best. Your commitment to excellence makes a difference.
104–115	Your impact is good, and you're probably achieving fine results. Remember, today "good" isn't good enough.
103 and below	Competition is tough today and challenges are massive. Often the difference between winning and losing is small. Use this opportunity to rise above the crowd and excel. Go for it. You haven't any time to lose.

40
55
20
115

DEVELOP YOUR HUMAN SKILLS

As an employee, your productivity was measured and compared with your co-workers. Your supervisor probably did this through some kind of performance evaluation and formal review. Your promotion may have depended on these reviews.

When you become a supervisor, you are measured by the productivity of your team; and your future depends on how well your team performs. If you employ the human skills that motivate your employees to produce more, you will be recognized for doing a good job. If the opposite happens, you will be recognized for doing a poor job.

You can contribute to productivity by handling a few tasks yourself. This practice also helps to set the work pace. If you do too much, however, your people may not get the supervision that will allow them to produce more. To test your understanding, please answer the following true or false questions. The correct answers are given below.

TRUE FALSE

❏ ❏ 1. Nothing should receive higher priority than helping an employee reach his or her productivity potential.

❏ ❏ 2. A drop in performance by a reliable employee need not be handled immediately, since other employees might resent the attention.

❏ ❏ 3. Employees will often produce more for one supervisor than for another.

❏ ❏ 4. A disruptive employee who reduces the performance of co-workers must be dealt with immediately.

❏ ❏ 5. Some employees with only modest personal productivity can help the productivity of others so much with their positive attitude that supervisors value them highly.

❏ ❏ 6. Most employees have a higher productivity potential than they realize.

TRUE FALSE

7. Generally speaking, the better employees perform, the better they feel about themselves.

8. Human skills are easier to learn than technical ones.

9. A think-smart supervisor can do less personally and still have the highest performing unit.

10. A "golden" employee is one who performs at a high level and contributes measurably to the productivity of co-workers.

Answers to exercises:

1. T 2. F 3. T 4. T 5. T 6. T 7. T 8. F 9. T 10. T

ESTABLISHING GOOD RELATIONSHIPS

Establishing and maintaining fair, open, and healthy relationships—including behavioral standards—is the key to good supervision. Define and communicate the behavioral standards that you expect all employees to maintain. Describe what is expected and what is not permitted.

Most employees enjoy working in an environment that has high but achievable standards. Workers feel more secure about their jobs when their supervisor takes control and does not permit one employee to get by with recognized violations.

It is important to set a reasonable and *consistent* discipline line. As you learn to do this, remember that you can show compassion and maintain high standards at the same time.

When Something Goes Wrong

In becoming a successful supervisor, you will make your share of human relations mistakes. Error is inevitable because each situation is different. However, if you permit mistakes to go uncorrected, you may become the victim if employees become offended and reduce productivity, start rumors, or are otherwise disruptive. You did not intend to damage a relationship, but you become the victim anyway. To avoid this situation, consider the following:

- Apologize and acknowledge the error.

- Talk to the injured parties so they can air their grievances. Communication is not only the best way to restore a relationship: often it is the only way.

THE PROBLEM EMPLOYEE

All supervisors must occasionally manage a difficult employee. Some employees are consistently late or absent from work. Others create false rumors that reduce productivity. Still others disobey rules or make mistakes that need to be corrected. In extreme cases, problem employees carry hostility toward another employee or manager.

How you manage such employees and convert them into team members is a critical part of your job. The following suggestions are designed to provide you with the help you may need.

From Trouble to Teammate: A 10-Item Quiz

Below are 10 ways to react to an employee who is demanding, hostile, and disruptive. *Three are acceptable forms of behavior.* Place a check in the box next to those you feel are appropriate behaviors for a supervisor. Then match your answers with those at the bottom of the page. Remember, we are talking about your initial reaction—not action that might be taken later.

1. Stay cool. Let the employee express anger without an immediate reaction on your part.

2. Let the employee know that you consider him or her to be a problem.

3. Challenge the employee in a stern manner.

4. Consider the employee as objectively as possible and refuse to take things personally.

5. Avoid the problem. Time will solve it.

6. Become distant and noncommunicative.

7. Challenge the employee to stop giving you a problem.

8. Act uninterested and ignore the situation.

9. Get angry and return the kind of behavior you receive.

10. In a calm manner say: "Let's talk in my office."

Firm, friendly, and *fair* are the key words in maintaining your disciplinary line. When a difficult situation arises, it is time to use your coaching and counseling skills.

Answers to exercise: 1, 4, 10

SIX UNFORGIVABLE MISTAKES

1. Treating individuals unequally because of sex, culture, age, or educational background. Each employee is unique and should receive the same consideration as any other.

2. Breaking trust with an employee. The fastest way to destroy a relationship is to make a promise and then break it.

3. Changing your mind, attitude, or approach without reason. Consistency is essential when supervising. If you are positive one day and negative the next, employees will not know how to react. Respect will disappear.

4. Failing to follow basic company policies and procedures. As a supervisor, you must handle your relationship with each employee in a fair and legal manner. This may mean, for example, establishing an improvement plan before you ask for approval to terminate an employee.

5. Losing your cool in front of others. Everyone reaches his or her threshold of tolerance occasionally; but, as a supervisor, you need to keep your temper in check. Blowing up can destroy relationships.

6. Engaging in a personal relationship with someone you supervise. When you become a supervisor, you change your role. It is poor policy to be in charge of a person during the day and personally involved with him or her after work.

Review

In as few words as possible, rewrite the six unforgivable mistakes in your own words.

1. _____

2. _____

3. _____

4. _____

5. _____

6. _____

LEADERS BUILD WINNING TEAMS

Some supervisors seem content with the status quo. They like their group and its performance. They may not have thought beyond what is accomplished to what might be achieved under slightly different circumstances. Other supervisors, however, using the same number of people doing similar tasks, can improve productivity dramatically. They have established a climate where employees are willing to give their best and work together in teams.

A comparison of teams and groups is shown on the next page. Check the characteristics representative of your team.

GROUPS VERSUS TEAMS

☐ Members think they are grouped together for administrative purposes only. Individuals work independently, sometimes at cross purposes with others.

☐ Members recognize their interdependence and understand that both personal and team goals are best accomplished with mutual support. Time is not wasted struggling over "turf" or attempting personal gain at the expense of others.

☐ Members focus on themselves because they are not sufficiently involved in planning the team's objectives. They approach their jobs with a "hired hand" mentality.

☐ Members feel committed to their jobs and unit because they are committed to goals they helped to establish.

☐ Members are told what to do rather than asked what the best approach would be. Suggestions are not encouraged.

☐ Members contribute to the team's success by applying their unique talents and knowledge to team objectives.

☐ Members distrust the motives of colleagues because they do not understand the roles of other members. Expressions of opinion or disagreement are considered divisive or nonsupportive.

☐ Members work in a climate of trust and are encouraged to express ideas, opinions, disagreements, and feelings. Questions are welcomed.

☐ Members are so cautious about what they say that real understanding is not possible.

☐ Members practice open and honest communication. They make an effort to understand each other's perspective.

☐ Members may receive good training but cannot fully apply it to the job.

☐ Members are encouraged to develop skills and apply what they learn on the job. They receive the support of the team.

☐ Members find themselves in conflict situations that they do not know how to resolve. Their supervisor may put off intervention until serious damage is done.

☐ Members recognize conflict as a normal aspect of human interaction and view such situations as an opportunity for new ideas and creativity. They work to resolve conflict quickly and constructively.

☐ Members may or may not participate in decisions affecting the team. Conformity often appears more important than positive results.

☐ Members participate in decisions affecting the team but understand that their leader must make a final ruling whenever the team cannot decide or an emergency exists. Positive results, not conformity, are the goal.

TEAMS GROW IN STAGES

Any team evolves through a life cycle from birth to maturity. Each stage of the cycle has predictable transition characteristics. The supervisor who knows what to expect in these stages is better prepared to serve the employees' needs and help team members handle the situations inherent in each stage.

Since the early 1960s, team developers have identified these predictable stages of team development.

Stages of Team Development

TEAMS GROW IN STAGES (continued)

STAGE 1: FORMING

The *forming* stage represents the first steps of shifting individuals into a group. Most team members will not have worked in a group before and will not know what to expect. The team members' characteristics and suggested supervisor actions of this "feeling out" stage include:

Team Member Characteristics

- Hesitant participation tempered with optimism
- Complaints and gripes common
- Some suspicion and fear of team situation
- Looking for sense of belonging
- Closely watching the team members' behaviors

Supervisor Behaviors

- Ensure team members get acquainted
- Acknowledge team members' needs
- Offer clear direction and information
- Assign team simple tasks
- Provide intensive "awareness" training
- Provide training on team-building tools

STAGE 2: STORMING

In this stage the group evolves slowly, if at all. In fact, the *storming* stage has great downside possibilities if the supervisor does not counter these tendencies.

Team Member Characteristics

- Conflict between team members surfaces
- Egos flare

- Concern over team versus individual responsibilities arises

- Confusion about team members' roles continues

Supervisor Behaviors

- Continue to be positive and informative

- Reassure team members that conflict is normal

- Handle conflict openly

- Assign team more responsible tasks

- Continue to train on team building and team tools

STAGE 3: NORMING

In the *norming* stage the team begins to come together. Conflict is substantially reduced as the team grows in confidence and begins to find that the team concept is working.

Team Member Characteristics

- Over-reliance on supervisor possible

- Conflicts reduced among team members

- Sharing and discussing become team norms

- Greater team cohesiveness develops

- Harmony among team members becomes common

Supervisor Behaviors

- Provide less structure as team matures

- Give team even more responsibility

- Ensure team does not overly rely on any one member

- Continue to provide team development and training opportunities

TEAMS GROW IN STAGES (continued)

STAGE 4: PERFORMING

As maturity continues, *team* behavior becomes the norm. While team members may be occasionally replaced, the team has become self-functioning. The team routinely defines and solves more difficult issues.

Team Member Characteristics

- Intense loyalty among team members develops

- Teams may mask individual dysfunctional members

- Teams can become competitive with other teams

- Teams need greater information

- Teams become more innovative

- Team members become more confident

Supervisor Behaviors

- Ensure team's information needs are fulfilled

- Ensure that the team celebrates its successes

- Encourage team toward continued growth

- Continue to train; ensure new team members are properly trained

- Encourage team members to rotate roles

- Reduce your involvement as team grows

- Continue to foster trust and commitment among team members

STAGE 5: ADJOURNING

This final stage of team development occurs for teams that have a specified lifetime, when the team completes a major task or special event, or when several new team members are added to an existing team.

Team Member Characteristics

- Members feel a sense of accomplishment

- Teams measure their success against goals

- Members may feel sad or resentful that the team is disbanding or changing

Supervisor Behaviors

- Encourage evaluation of team's performance

- Recognize and reward team efforts

- Encourage ventilation of feelings

- Use ceremonies to bring a sense of closure to this phase of the team's development

TEAM DEVELOPMENT EXERCISE

Identify the following sentences relating to team development stages by place a **F** (Forming), **S** (Storming), **N** (Norming), or **P** (Performing) in the space provided. Check your answers with those in the box at the bottom of the page.

_____ 1. Conflict between team members surfaces.

_____ 2. Members look for a sense of belonging.

_____ 3. Organizational complaints and gripes are common.

_____ 4. Harmony among team members becomes common.

_____ 5. Team needs greater information.

_____ 6. Intense loyalty among team members develops.

_____ 7. Egos flare.

_____ 8. Sharing and discussing become team norms.

_____ 9. Team can become competitive with other teams.

_____ 10. Some members express suspicion and fear of team situation.

_____ 11. Concern over team versus individual responsibilities develops.

_____ 12. Members may rely too much on supervisor.

Answers: 1. S, 2. F, 3. F, 4. N, 5. P, 6. P, 7. S, 8. N, 9. P, 10. F, 11. S, 12. N

CASE STUDY #3: Between a Rock and a Hard Place

Grace did so well as a supervisor that upper management invited her to attend an all-day management workshop. When she showed up for work the following day her boss, Mr. Adams, called her into his office and questioned her harshly about the behavior of her employees. Knowing Grace was absent, Mr. Adams had dropped by her office and found her employees talking and laughing loudly. Grace, feeling let down by her staff, told Mr. Adams it would not happen again and on the following day came down hard on everyone at a meeting. Then, after checking the situation, Grace discovered that it was one of her employees' birthday and a few of their customers had stopped by to wish the employee a happy birthday. Mr. Adams had misinterpreted the situation.

How, in your opinion, should Grace handle the situation? Write your answer below.

_____

_____

_____

_____

_____

_____

For author's comments on this case study turn to page 77.

KEEPING THE BOSS HAPPY

As a supervisor it is important not only to keep your employees happy and productive, it is also important to make sure that good relationships are maintained with your management. Don't forget: you are the buffer and must be concerned with relationships in both directions.

Here are three suggestions to assist you in developing and maintaining a healthy, open relationship with *your* boss.

1. **Tie your team goals to those of your department/district/division.**

Listen to changes that come down from above and bring your team into alignment. Keep communications open to your management. Know their priorities and plans, so you can tie your work efforts to support them.

2. **Keep your boss informed.**

Share the good news (it is a good idea to have upper management compliment one of your deserving employees now and then) and openly admit any misjudgments you may have made.

3. **Be a good team member.**

As a supervisor, you will need to build good relationships with supervisors and management other than your immediate boss. In doing this, see that your boss is placed in the best possible light with others. Do this even though she or he may not give you all the recognition you feel you deserve.

S E C T I O N

IV

Getting the Work Done

DELEGATING IS GOOD FOR EVERYBODY

Delegating—assigning tasks to others—has two enormous benefits. It reduces your own task load, and it helps employees make their best contribution to the productivity of your team. When you delegate, you become a teacher. You tell an employee how to perform a new task, show how it is done, and then ask your employee to demonstrate the task that has been learned. Delegating takes time, patience, and follow-up to ensure that the delegated task is done right.

As a supervisor you must learn how to distribute tasks evenly, tap the special creativity of each individual, and, when appropriate, rotate responsibilities among employees. Try to capitalize on the ideas of your employees, even when it means taking a risk. Proper delegation keeps employees motivated, increases productivity, and frees the supervisor to do his or her own work.

CASE STUDY #4: *The Do-It-Yourself Supervisor*

Joanne was a capable and enthusiastic employee. She was promoted to supervise a group of 10 employees doing work very similar to her own past assignment.

She began her new position thinking, "I was promoted because of my excellent performance. Therefore, I must have greater expertise than any of my employees and can probably complete most of the reports better and faster than they can. I will train them when I have time, but right now I had better concentrate on getting the work done."

Joanne did not pass on any major assignments to her employees; she did most of the reports herself. As time passed, her hours of work increased steadily and she was less and less available to her employees, peers, and to her own manager—with whom coordination was important. Her employees were given only the most routine work and received no training. One resigned because of the lack of challenge and personal growth. Joanne was too busy to replace him. Finally, after 60 days, Joanne's manager called her in to discuss her performance.

What would you have said to Joanne if you had been her manager? Please summarize your comments below.

_____

_____

_____

_____

_____

For author's comments on this case study turn to page 78.

WHAT DELEGATING CAN DO FOR YOU

Supervisors like Joanne in Case Study #4 often assign a low priority to delegation because they are unsure of how to go about it and don't see the benefits. Some think delegation is more trouble than it's worth. Some advantages of good delegation are listed below. Check those you would like to achieve.

❑ More work can be accomplished and deadlines can be met more easily.

❑ Employees become involved and committed.

❑ Assigning responsibility and authority makes employee control less difficult.

❑ Employees grow and develop.

❑ Human resources are more fully utilized and productivity improves.

❑ Individual performance can be measured more accurately.

❑ Compensation, including merit increases, can be more directly related to individual performance.

❑ A diversity of products, operations, and people can be managed effectively.

❑ Employee satisfaction and recognition are enhanced.

❑ More time is available for planning, organizing, and motivating.

❑ Freedom to do those tasks only I, as manager, can do.

Please add any other advantages you can think of in the spaces below.

_____

_____

_____

D-E-L-E-G-A-T-E
FOR BETTER PERFORMANCE

D escribe the project or task to be delegated.

E xplain the reason for delegating the project or task to the employee.

L et the employee ask questions.

E xplain the resources available: time, budget, labor, and so on.

G et the employee's suggestions for completing the assignment.

A ddress the employee's suggestions, questions, and concerns.

T ake time to check in on the employee's progress.

E mpower the employee to make decisions with your support.

DECIDE WHAT TO DELEGATE

> **Any time you perform a task someone else could do, you keep yourself from a task only you can do.**

Supervisors usually delegate in order to give themselves more time to do management tasks, improve productivity, or develop their employees. Some types of work you should consider delegating are listed below.

► **Decisions you make most frequently.**

Minor decisions and repetitive routines often consume a major portion of the day. Most, if not all, of these can be delegated by teaching employees the policies and procedures that apply. They probably already know the details better than you.

List two possibilities:

1. _____

2. _____

► **Tasks that are in your technical or functional speciality.**

These are usually operating tasks rather than supervisory functions. You can teach others to do them. In fact, your challenge as a supervisor is to motivate others to produce better results than you ever did as an individual performer. Part of the time you save can be used to learn about other functions you supervise, so you can manage them better.

List two possibilities:

1. _____

2. _____

DECIDE WHAT TO DELEGATE (continued)

▶ **Tasks and projects for which you are least qualified.**

Some of your employees are almost certainly better qualified and can do part of the job better than you. Let them.

List two possibilities:

1. _____

2. _____

▶ **Functions you dislike.**

Performing functions we dislike is distasteful, and we often put them off or do them poorly. Examine the likes and dislikes of your staff as well as their talents. You will nearly always find someone who likes the job and can do it well. If they need training, provide it.

List two possibilities:

1. _____

2. _____

▶ **Work that provides experience for employees.**

Make growth in the present job a reality and keep employees challenged and motivated.

List two possibilities:

1. _____

2. _____

▶ **Assignments that add variety to routine work.**

A change of pace is usually welcome and often a good motivator for an employee whose job is growing dull.

List two possibilities:

1. _____

2. _____

► **Activities that make a position more complete.**

As employees become more proficient, they often look for the next challenge. Add complementary duties and responsibilities to give their positions more substance but ensure the regular duties are covered.

List two possibilities:

1. _____

2. _____

► **Tasks that increase the number of people who can perform critical assignments.**

Maximize the strength of the group by giving people the experience to back up one another during emergencies or periods of unusually heavy work.

List two possibilities:

1. _____

2. _____

► **Opportunities to use and reinforce creative talents.**

Employees are not creative in a stifling environment. Stimulate them with difficult problems and projects, and reward creative solutions.

List two possibilities:

1. _____

2. _____

DEVELOP YOUR DECISION-MAKING SKILLS

How well do you make decisions? Maybe you're doing great, or maybe you need to improve. See where you fit on the scale. Read the statement at both ends of the scale and then circle the number that best indicates where you belong.

When making an important decision, I consider how it fits our mission.	5 4 3 2 1	It's too difficult to consider our mission when making important decisions.
My employees see consistency in my decisions.	5 4 3 2 1	There's very little consistency in my decisions.
I feel comfortable making a decision without all related data.	5 4 3 2 1	I must have as much data as possible to make a decision.
I am careful not to overwhelm myself with information when making a decision.	5 4 3 2 1	I often feel overwhelmed by the data when making a decision.
I make timely decisions.	5 4 3 2 1	I procrastinate when decisions are important.
I communicate my decisions to those who will be affected.	5 4 3 2 1	I neglect or forget to tell people about decisions that may affect them.
I stay up-to-date with industry and company trends.	5 4 3 2 1	I'm too busy to worry about industry and company trends.
I delegate problems to employees that they can and should solve.	5 4 3 2 1	I make most of the decisions.
I am committed to developing my employees so they can make more and better decisions.	5 4 3 2 1	My employees would prefer me to make the decisions.
When a decision is complex, I follow a logical formula.	5 4 3 2 1	When a decision is complex, I muddle through as best I can.

TOTAL ☐

If you scored 40–50, you are an outstanding decision maker on all important fronts. If you scored 30–39, you are very good at decision-making and involve the appropriate individuals. If you scored 20–29, you are doing well, but may want to look at the answers you checked for areas you can improve upon even more. If you scored below 20, you may want to develop a decision-making plan.

Portrait of a Decision

You may remember the Tylenol® poisoning scare that happened several years ago. Some people who had taken Tylenol® died, and no one knew why. James Burke, the chief executive officer of Johnson & Johnson, faced one of the toughest decisions of his life. Should he pull Tylenol® from all the stores?

The financial cost would be enormous. The legal implications could be staggering. His decision: pull the product.

Burke attributes his decision to the values outlined in Johnson & Johnson's mission statement: "We believe our first responsibility is to the doctors, nurses and patients, to mothers and all others who use our products and services." Burke is a clear example of a leader who knew his mission and used it to make decisions. Johnson & Johnson did suffer financially that year, but it came back stronger than ever with more customer trust than it could have bought with millions of dollars of advertising.

KNOWING WHEN TO HOLD AND WHEN TO FOLD

Judiciousness is another big card in your leadership poker hand. Obviously you want to make the best possible decision in the most efficient way. Some supervisors demand all the financial data, historical information, management opinion, customer feedback, and more. By the time all this data is gathered, it is either too late or overwhelming. The results are inconsistent. This type of decision-making leads to poor decisions at best and paralysis at worst.

How do you make decisions if you can't know everything? First, you must stay current on industry trends. You need to look for patterns of growth, opportunities, and problems. Leaders continuously work to anticipate the future, rather than react to it. Certainly there may be some data you must have, or some individuals (such as your boss) whose support is absolutely necessary. But the challenge of leadership is judging when you have enough information so that you are not shooting from the hip, and not waiting so long that the strategic moment has passed. Leaders often talk about making "gut" decisions. Although this may sound unusual, what they are really talking about is understanding the situation without getting lost in the data.

One reality of decision-making is that you will, at times, make the wrong decision. Consider mistakes lesson in your school of leadership. You won't do your job perfectly every time. Fifty-one percent of making the right decision is in taking a step in the right direction.

CASE STUDY #5: Pat Can't Decide

Pat dreamed of the day he would become a supervisor. He looked forward to calling the shots and making the decisions. Pat enjoys an information system of reports, data, projections, and the history of just about every element of his job to help him make the right decision.

Much to his surprise, Pat finds his stomach in knots when it's time to decide. He wonders if he should look at the data differently. Should he ask for an additional report? Should he talk to his manager? Should he do more research? Should he read another article? He wants to make the right decision, and suddenly it seems as if there is no right decision.

Lately, Pat has noticed that his employees seem to be kidding him about whether decisions have been made yet. Even his boss has made some remarks. The problem is, he's just not sure if all of the factors have been considered.

What would you coach Pat to do?

_____

_____

_____

_____

_____

_____

See page 78 for the author's recommendation.

USING A FORMULA FOR DECISION-MAKING

Some decisions are simple and the answers are obvious. Others are complex and require you to weigh many factors. At times it's not even clear what the problems or issues are that have to be solved.

Having a formula to help you sort through a situation can help you look at factors and identify your best options. The formula below is designed to help make decision making more methodical.

 **Define desired outcome.**

You need to know what you want to accomplish before you can decide the best way to do it.

 **Establish decision criteria.**

What are the guidelines? For example, if you were deciding whether to assign work to one of your employees or to outsource it, you would consider factors like workload, cost, or time savings. What people or processes will be affected?

 **Consider alternative solutions.**

Write out all possible courses of action that could lead to the desirable outcome.

STEP #4 **Investigate.**

Accumulate as many facts as time permits. List them on a separate sheet of paper.

 **Determine the top three choices.**

Narrow your choices to the best three. List them.

STEP #6   **Initiate a comparison.**

Weigh the three choices and decide among them. Consult with others if necessary.

STEP #7   **Opt for the best choice.**

List your final decision. Keep a reference of the other two paths. You need them later as Plans B and C.

STEP #8   **Announce your decision with conviction.**

The way you articulate your decision can be as important as the quality of the decision itself. Write out how you intend to announce it.

STEP #9   **See that the decision is fully implemented.**

A good decision must be made to work. Write out how you intend to do this.

FREEING YOURSELF TO LEAD

You can't be a true leader sensing the environment for trends and focusing on the long haul if you are bogged down in the daily detail of decision-making. If employees need to come to you for every approval, the decision-making process needs to be pushed to a lower level.

Consider how many decisions, large and small, you make in a day. Could or should others be shouldering part of this load? Often supervisors are reluctant to let go of decision making. Following are some of the common reasons. Check those you feel are true of you.

❏ I can decide faster alone.

❏ I would lose control if I didn't make the decisions.

❏ I know all the factors; my employees don't.

❏ The employee might make a mistake.

❏ I have more experience and therefore can make better decisions.

❏ I feel guilty asking the employees to make the decision when it's my responsibility.

❏ My employees don't like making decisions and want me to decide.

❏ I like making all the decisions.

If any of the above sounds like you, it's time to change. You can't be a leader if you are involved in every day-to-day decision. If you feel your employees are unprepared to handle decisions on their own, then prepare them. If they don't have the background, make sure they get it. If they don't have the confidence, work with them. Praise their good decisions. If they put it back on your plate, refuse to accept it. Leaders cannot be involved in the daily load of details.

Where you must focus your decision-making energy is on those issues that set the direction of your responsibilities. You must be at the forefront in any decision that will have a long-term impact.

DECISION PYRAMID—LEVELS OF DECISION-MAKING

Empowered decision-making can happen at all levels, and each is appropriate at different times. The diagram below shows supervisor and team member responsibilities at all levels.

Supervisor	Level	Team Member
Define process and criteria by which decisions are to be reached. Embrace the decisions.	**5** **Delegate**	Accept responsibility for decision-making process.
Participate in and acknowledge consensual process.	**4** **Collaboration**	Work on outcome until it feels right. Embrace the decision.
Listen and discuss participant's input. Make decision.	**3** **Dialogue**	Active participation, voice opinions. Suport decision.
Listen to input. Make clear decision.	**2** **Input**	Voice opinions at the time.
Give a direct command.	**1** **Directive**	Listen carefully.

FOUR COMPONENTS OF DECISIONS

Many qualified employees refuse opportunities to become supervisors because they do not want to face the problem-solving responsibilities that go with the job. Some of these individuals are not aware that there are proven techniques to help them make good decisions.

Once you have learned the problem-solving techniques, how quickly you move forward will be shaped by the decisions you make. Success or failure is usually based on the quality of our decisions.

Four important components of leadership decisions are:

1. *BEING TRUE TO YOUR MISSION:* **Where It Will Take You**

Your mission is your beacon, your guiding light. It underlies all your decisions and gives your leadership consistency. Your employees may not agree with all of your decisions, but if they see the consistency behind them, they can support and follow.

2. *THE FORMULA:* **How**

When you make dozens of decisions every day, it is very easy to act immediately without thinking or planning. A few important steps in decision-making can improve your decisions.

3. *ANALYSIS PARALYSIS:* **When**

The information age has brought thousands of facts to our fingertips. You might think this leads to a better decision, but the opposite is often the case. The sheer amount of data can lead to analysis paralysis. Leaders must know how to make decisions without pouring over every bit of data.

4. *DECISIONS AT THE RIGHT LEVEL:* **Who**

Nothing can bog down a supervisor more quickly than trying to make all the decisions. It is not easy to delegate decisions to others who might not be as knowledgeable. It can be confusing to know which jobs are only yours to do. Most important in delegating decisions is choosing which jobs to delegate and then consistently delegating those to others.

SET DAILY GOALS

Planning is the thinking that precedes doing. Planning means setting goals for yourself and your employees that support larger company goals. Properly articulated, most employees respond positively to reachable goals, especially when employees have been involved in the goal-setting process and participate in the excitement when goals are reached.

Before you became a supervisor, chances are you could do your job without much serious planning. You basically reacted and adjusted to goals that had already been established. Your supervisor probably gave them to you. Now that you're the supervisor, a daily plan that can be reviewed and implemented *before* the workday begins is essential.

Supervisors are always planning. Planning goes with the territory. Most successful supervisors operate with a daily checklist. The smart ones:

✔ Keep a list of prioritized "to do" tasks.

✔ Use a star or other symbol to designate projects with the highest priority.

✔ Write daily goals in their personal notebook, planner, or desk calendar.

✔ Enjoy the process of drawing a line through goals as they are reached.

✔ Recognize and reward others who help reach significant goals.

Use your own system and select your own style, but supplement your long-term objectives with daily goals. It will make you feel much better on your way home each day.

SECTION

V

Review

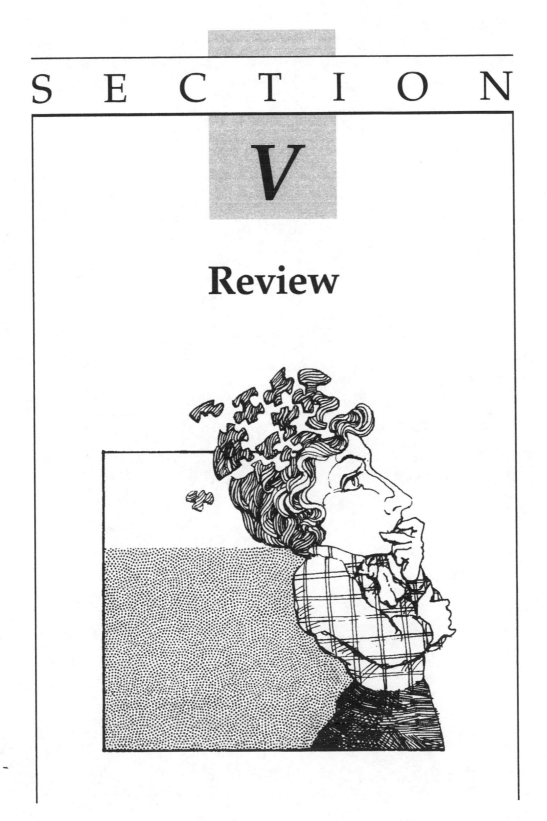

PUTTING IT TOGETHER

Throughout this book you have learned that being a successful supervisor is a combination of personal characteristics (positive attitude, confidence, patience, and so on) and the application of skills and techniques (delegating, developing your team, restoring relationships, and so on).

Can You Put All of These Requirements Together?

Of course you can—especially if you don't try to do everything at once. Remember that after everything is accomplished the measure of your success as a supervisor is how well you achieve improved productivity.

If your team of employees is regularly recognized for higher productivity than similar teams, management will recognize this and you will enhance your own skills, abilities, and career.

Achieving greater productivity is a human challenge. As a supervisor, it is not what you can accomplish by doing tasks yourself, but the quality of the working relationships you build with the employees who do the work for you.

Good Luck!

Supervising for Success

Review your notes from previous chapters and create an Action Plan of how you will apply the training concepts from each of the sections to your position.

LESSONS LEARNED   **APPLICATION**

Section I: A Role Defined

_____   _____

_____   _____

_____   _____

Section II: The Attitude and Image

_____   _____

_____   _____

_____   _____

Section III: Human Skills and Team Building

_____   _____

_____   _____

_____   _____

Section IV: Getting the Work Done

_____   _____

_____   _____

_____   _____

AUTHOR'S COMMENTS ON CASE STUDIES

CASE STUDY #1

Who Will Survive?, *page 7*

Both Tom and Chris will most likely survive as supervisors. Tom will probably be better liked as a supervisor. Chris, however, will probably earn more respect. Tom may be too casual in learning the many techniques and principles every supervisor should learn. Tom may be very effective onsite and in his new position. If he wants to advance in management, he may want to research more about leadership and management beyond his current environment. Chris, on the other hand, may want to focus less on her transition and work more closely with her group.

CASE STUDY #2

Which Strategy Should Henry Use?, *page 24*

We favor Strategy 2 but would also follow up the group session with individual coaching to avoid any misunderstandings and to improve relationships. Henry should not expect 100% compliance to his new standards quickly. He should, however, set his standards high enough to achieve the kind of productivity desired. Reachable standards are required, but employees should be given sufficient time to reach them. While doing this, Henry should also set a good example both as a supervisor and an employee.

CASE STUDY #3

Between a Rock and a Hard Place, *page 51*

First Grace should go to Mr. Adams and explain the reason for her employees' behavior and stand up for them and their normally high productivity. Second, she should tell her employees what happened at the meeting with Mr. Adams. A supervisor's first responsibility is to go to bat for his or her employees.

AUTHOR'S COMMENTS ON CASE STUDIES (continued)

CASE STUDY #4

The Do-It-Yourself Supervisor, page 65

Joanne's manager didn't waste time getting to the point. She simply asked her to talk about her workload and that of her employees. The contrast made the problem obvious. When Joanne explained her rationale, the manager disagreed. She suggested Joanne take a good look at her employees and their past work record. Most were high achievers when given the chance. She suggested that Joanne was afraid to let go of responsibility and authority and perhaps enjoyed doing work more than managing it. Joanne then admitted that perhaps she didn't know how to let go and still maintain control. The discussion concluded with Joanne agreeing to attend a seminar on delegating and to work closely with her manager when she was unsure of how to proceed.

CASE STUDY #5

Pat Can't Decide, page 65

Pat needs to design a decision-making formula that is comfortable for him to use and one in which he can have confidence. After doing this, he needs to remind himself that: (1) All decisions are calculated risks, (2) Decisions can usually be reversed without damage to the image of the leader, (3) Nobody maintains a decision "track record" on Pat, and (4) Making no decision can be the worst decision of all.